FAITH
FOR
OUR TIMES

Contemporary Prayers,

Poetry and Prose

Edited by Karen Middaugh

♛ Hallmark Editions

WE CAN'T MAKE IT ALONE, LORD

God knows, we've tried, and we've even reached the point where we could blow up everybody, including ourselves. Teach us how to listen carefully and patiently to other people. Teach us how to say what we have to say clearly, simply, and openly. Teach us what responsibility toward you and others really means.

Cut through all our egoism and self-interest, Jesus. Make us understand what patriotism must mean in one world of conflicting nationalisms. Educate us to support the United Nations and other international organizations which bring people together in a shared sense of human concern. Work with us, Lord, to bridge gulfs and divisions between nations and persons.

MALCOLM BOYD

COMING TO TERMS WITH FAITH

Once I heard a man say: "I spent twenty years trying to come to terms with my doubts. Then one day it dawned on me that I had better come to terms with my faith. Now I have passed from the agony of questions I cannot answer into the agony of answers I cannot escape. And it's a great relief."

DAVID E. ROBERTS

5

RITE OF RECONCILIATION

Let us confess our sins to each other and to God,
our merciful father.
Lord, we have remained cool
to the fire of your word;
we have not dared to live for others.
    Lord have mercy.
Lord, we have failed as your peacemakers;
we have continued to live by violence,
in our homes, our cities and our country.
    Lord have mercy.

Lord, we have refused your freedom;
we have remained trapped
within our narrow prejudices,
in the closed circles
of the safe and the comfortable.
    Lord have mercy.
Lord, we have failed to love;
we have turned from those who love us,
and chosen not to see those who need us.
    Lord have mercy.

Father, we confess and repent these and all
    the sins by which we have turned away
        from each other and from you
    in our thinking, speaking and doing.
    We have done the evil you forbid,

and have not done the good to which
   we are called.
Our lives and our society are twisted,
   narrow and violent,
and the guilt for this is ours.
We do repent, and we are truly sorry
   for all our sins.
Have mercy on us, kind Father,
because of the obedience of our brother Jesus,
   your son.
Forgive us all we have done, and not done,
and help us to forgive one another.
Confirm our repentance with the power
   of your spirit;
move us now to live for each other and for you
so that we may build a just
   and peaceful society
and live the new life you offer us,
   through Jesus Christ, our Lord. Amen.
Our God is a loving father.
He forgives those who repent and turn to him.
May he forgive you your sins, strengthen your
repentance, and open to you the fullness
of his life, through Jesus Christ, our Lord.
       Amen.

     from THE UNDERGROUND MASS BOOK

from TO BELIEVE IN GOD

One by one our old heavens
have left us
places in hearts all we have left
we cannot live forever
outside each other
who still dream of mansions.
To believe in God
is to get high
on love enough
to look down
at your loneliness and
forget it forever.

JOSEPH PINTAURO

THE CHURCH RENEWED

The church is dropping its old skin, Lord.
Have you noticed?
It had grown flabby from guarding its treasure
    instead of healthy from running to give it away.
Please allow it to hang loose until it's free from
    growing pains and help us realize that before
    it can be frisky in the fields of service, Lord,
    it has to be free of its old skin.
            Amen

JEANETTE STRUCHEN

8

SCIENCE AND GOD

There are those, I know . . . who will object that Job's story bears no relationship to our own because God has changed in the interval. The God of Job is God the Creator of the Universe, and science, they say, now knows that there is no such Creator . . . that the watch winds itself. . . .

I have no wish and certainly no competence to argue the questions of faith. . . . But two things may be said. . . . Einstein has told us that he had sometimes the sense that he was following . . . the track of an Intelligence far beyond the reaches of his own. The second thing to be said is this: that there has been nothing in human history that has brought mankind closer to . . . infinite creativity than the revelation that the minutest particles of inert matter contain an almost immeasurable power.

ARCHIBALD MAC LEISH

KEEP ME AT IT

God, give me due respect for the abilities you
have given me.

Don't let me sell them short. Don't let me
cheapen them. Don't let me bury my talents
through indecision, cowardice, or laziness.

Plant in me the necessary determination.
Keep me at it.

Rouse in me the fires of dedication. Keep
me at it.

Give me the energy, strength and willpower
to bring your gifts to their proper fruition.
Keep me at it.

When I falter or fall lift me up and set
me back on my destined path. Keep me at it.

Oh, God, when the way seems dark
and there is no light there, plant at least
one small signal fire at the end of the long
black tunnel that I may keep plodding
steadily forward toward it.

When friends laugh at me, keep me at it.

When people tempt me away from it, keep
me at it.

When others scorn what I have produced,
let me not be discouraged. Keep me at it.

When those who have tried and failed
or who have never tried at all, those
who are envious or indolent, when such people

would hurt me by spiteful words or acts,
let me not be bothered. Return me to my task.
Keep me at it.

   Let nothing really matter but these precious
gifts you have entrusted to me. For their sake
let me be willing and proud to make
the sacrifice. Keep me at it.

MARJORIE HOLMES

THE FACE OF CHRIST

The tragic beauty of the face of Christ
shines in the face of man;

the abandoned old live on
in shabby rooms, far from inner comfort.
Outside, in the street
din and purpose, the world like a fiery animal
reined in by youth. Within
a pallid tiring heart
shuffles about its dwelling.

Nothing, or so little, come of life's promise.
Out of broken men, despised minds
what does one make —
a roadside show, a graveyard of the heart?

The Christian God reproves
faithless ranting minds
crushing like upper and lower stones
all life between;
Christ, fowler of street and hedgerow
of cripples and the distempered old
—eyes blind as woodknots,
tongues tight as immigrants' —
takes in His gospel net
all the hue and cry of existence.
Heaven, of such imperfection,
wary, ravaged, wild?

Yes. Compel them in.

DANIEL BERRIGAN

from "CHRISTMAS GREETING TO THE AMERICAN DREAM"

. . . May your balance grow fat and your waist
  stay lean.
May your clothes be fit for a king and queen.
May your photos appear in a magazine.
May you sleep in bliss, may you wake in beauty.
May you be excused from jury duty,
For having to be, or to work for, The Boss,
And from Clotho, Lachesis, and Atropos.
May you always be long when the market is up,
And short when it's down. If you keep the pup
The kids are sleeping with, may it grow
To take best of breed, and best of show.
May your luck leave even you bemused,
Your tax be rebated, your rent reduced.
May your loves be lyric, your health dramatic,
Your tenor, in general, light-operatic.
May your mind, like your kitchen, be automatic
And, never thinking, never be wrong,
But filled to the brim with piped-in song,
A hundred and seventy million strong,
Lurching a little, but marching along
To the rainbow's end, to the golden pot,
Till you get it — whether it's there or not.

JOHN CIARDI

from "LITANY FROM
THE UNDERGROUND, I"

O God, who is three and whose belly aches in hunger,
    Help us to touch you.
O God, whose toys are broken bottles, tin cans,
whose play-yard is garbage and debris, and whose
playhouse is the floors of the condemned buildings,
    Help us to touch you.
O God, who sleeps in bed with his four brothers
and sisters, and who cries and no one hears him,
    Help us to touch you.
O God, who has no place to sleep tonight except
an abandoned car, some alley or deserted building,
    Help us to touch you.
O God, who is uneducated, unskilled, unwanted,
and unemployed,
    Help us to know you.
O God, who was laid off last week and can't pay
the rent or feed the kids,
    Help us to be with you.

ROBERT W. CASTLE, JR.

CHRIST CLIMBED DOWN

Christ climbed down
from His bare Tree
this year
and ran away to where
there were no rootless Christmas trees
hung with candycanes and breakable stars

Christ climbed down
from His bare Tree
this year
and ran away to where
there were no gilded Christmas trees
and no tinsel Christmas trees
and no tinfoil Christmas trees
and no pink plastic Christmas trees
and no gold Christmas trees
and no powderblue Christmas trees
hung with electric candles
and encircled by tin electric trains
and clever cornball relatives

Christ climbed down
from His bare Tree
this year
and ran away to where
no Bing Crosby carollers
groaned of a tight Christmas
and where no Radio City angels

iceskated wingless
thru a winter wonderland
into a jinglebell heaven
daily at 8:30
with Midnight Mass matinees

Christ climbed down
from His bare Tree
this year
and softly stole away into
some anonymous Mary's womb again
where in the darkest night
of everybody's anonymous soul
He awaits again
an unimaginable
and impossibly
Immaculate Reconception
the very craziest
of Second Comings

LAWRENCE FERLINGHETTI

JOIN IN THE DANCE

What is serious to men is often very trivial in the sight of God. What in God might appear to us as "play" is perhaps what He Himself takes most seriously. At any rate the Lord plays and diverts Himself in the garden of His creation, and if we could let go of our own obsession with what we think is the meaning of it all, we might be able to hear His call and follow Him in His mysterious, cosmic dance. We do not have to go very far to catch echoes of that game, and of that dancing. When we are alone on a starlit night; when by chance we see the migrating birds in autumn descending on a grove of junipers to rest and eat; when we see children in a moment when they are really children; when we know love in our own hearts; or when, like the Japanese poet Basho, we hear an old frog land in a quiet pond with a solitary splash — at such times the awakening, the turning inside out of all values, the "newness," the emptiness and the purity of vision that make themselves evident, provide a glimpse of the cosmic dance.

For the world and time are the dance of the Lord in emptiness. The silence of the spheres is the music of a wedding feast. The more we persist in misunderstanding the phenomena of life, the more we analyze them out into strange finalities and complex purposes of our own, the more we involve ourselves in sadness, absurdity and despair. But it does not matter much, because no despair of ours can alter the reality of things, or stain the joy of the cosmic dance which is always there. Indeed, we are in the midst of it, and it is in the midst of us, for it beats in our very blood, whether we want it to or not.

Yet the fact remains that we are invited to forget ourselves on purpose, cast our awful solemnity to the winds and join in the general dance.

THOMAS MERTON

ALL IS IN GOD

Lovers or friends desire two things. The one is to love each other so much that they enter into each other and only make one being. The other is to love each other so much that, with half the globe between them, their union will not be diminished in the slightest degree. All that man vainly desires here below is perfectly realized in God. We have all those impossible desires within us as a mark of our destination and they are good for us when we no longer hope to accomplish them.

SIMONE WEIL

JESUS UNSAVES

"Brother, are you saved?"

Most of us are at a loss for words if we're ever asked this question. One reaction is: "Saved from what?" It could be salvation from further thinking or inquiry. A neat formula about Jesus is not the same as faith in the living God.

When an architectural student is "saved" by Frank Lloyd Wright and becomes solely devoted to that style, he usually stunts his own creativity. If a writer tries to compose sentences exactly like Ernest Hemingway's, he will not discover his own true talent.

Actually, Jesus "unsaves" us from slavishly imitating anyone, including himself. Jesus calls men to be his disciples, not his robots. Being a Christian doesn't mean dressing like Jesus, or being single and a carpenter. It involves being ourselves and caring and sacrificing in our own situation as Jesus did in his.

This relationship to Jesus is quite different from freezing him into a formula.

ROBERT M. HERHOLD

THE MEANING OF LIFE

What is the meaning of human life, or, for that matter, of the life of any creature? To know an answer to this question means to be religious. You ask: Does it make any sense, then, to pose this question? I answer: The man who regards his own life and that of his fellow creatures as meaningless is not merely unhappy but hardly fit for life. . . .

The man of science . . . suffers a truly tragic fate. Striving in great sincerity for clarity and inner independence, he himself, through his sheer superhuman efforts, has fashioned the tools which are being used to make him a slave and to destroy him also from within. He cannot escape being muzzled by those who have the political power in their hands. As a soldier he is forced to sacrifice his own life and to destroy the lives of others even when he is convinced of the absurdity of such sacrifices . . . . [The scientist's] religious feeling takes the form of a rapturous amazement at the harmony of natural law, which reveals an intelligence of such superiority that, compared with it, all the systematic thinking and acting of human beings is an utterly insignificant reflection. . . .

ALBERT EINSTEIN

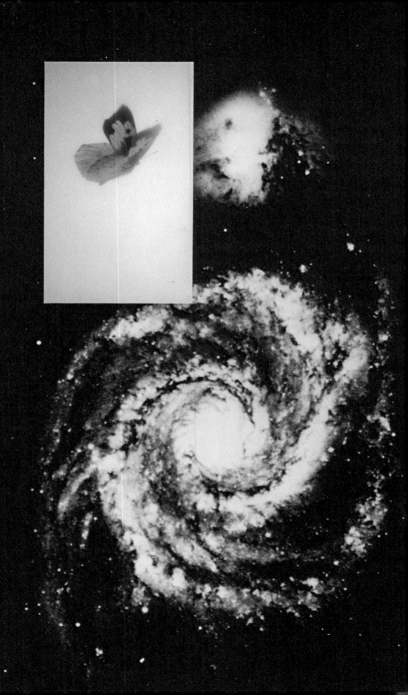

WHAT IS MAN?

A famous Nineteenth Century scientist once said that he did not believe in "the soul" because he could not find it in his test-tube. But surely, had the soul existed, a test-tube would be the last place where one would be likely to discover it, and the fallacy of that chemist's argument runs through most Nineteenth-Century science. Naturally it found only what its methods were capable of detecting and its faulty logic ran like this: "What my methods cannot investigate is not science; what science cannot investigate is not worth thinking about; what is not worth thinking about does not exist." It convinced the world simply because it dealt so successfully with what it could deal with.

Justice Oliver Wendell Holmes once declared that science teaches us a great deal about things that are not really very important; philosophy a very little about things that are of very great importance. This is indeed a very unfortunate fact, but not so unfortunate as the further fact that we forget the second half of Holmes' statement. . . .

Since man first began to think conceptually he has carried on . . . with the great questions arising out of the fact that he had indeed become Man; that he has seemingly unique desires, needs, hopes and fears. He invented what no other creature seemed capable of, namely Ethics, Aesthetics, and the other branches of metaphysics. He asked; "What is Justice?" "What is Beauty?" "What is The Good Life?" And though he never reached final answers, though he arrived at many different and often incompatible ones, he continued to ask; and it was the asking which made him always recognizable as that very very special animal called a human being.

JOSEPH WOOD KRUTCH

WHEN YOU HAVE THE BLAHS

I feel blah, O Jesus! I can't quite put my finger on why but I just don't have the get-up-and-go to make it through the day. I don't go for this religion stuff; and I don't speak any fancy church language. That's why I didn't talk with you before this. But a guy at work noticed how I was acting and he told me that prayer helped him. Can you beat it? I haven't prayed since I was a kid! This guy said that even though things were changing in today's world, prayer is still in. I hope so, because if it isn't, I'm out! I can't lick this by myself. I need you more than I have realized. Fill the emptiness of my life, Lord Jesus, as you seem to have done for my friend. Give me an injection of enthusiasm for life so I'll be worth something. Kick me in the pants if you have to; but help me out!

ORLANDO L. TIBBETTS

THINK OF JESUS

On His way to the city
to rid all people of the disease of complexity.
The earth was diseased with complexity.
The spirit had found print.
The law of the spirit was being formed
into words and sentences
and explanations and volumes
under the title: The Law of the Letter.
The simple script was diseased with the
    complexity of the law.
Law and rules for simple life
were spelled out,
divided,
subdivided,
catalogued,
categorized,
added,
multiplied,

until the simple way of life
was in long lists and columns
and was sick with complexity.
Laws had blinded the sight of people
and their common denominator.
They needed to hear the mathematician of Nazareth
say then
and forever —
600 Sabbath laws equal one law;
ten commandments equal one commandment:
Love.

HERBERT BROKERING

SUFFER WITH LOVE!

If men lose the conviction of the worth of struggle, of sorrow, of tears, of anguish, and of human death itself, they suffer a great defeat. Then the pessimism is justified which favors that surge of desperation projected into modern psychology that arises from the question: Of what purpose is life if it is going to finish in such a way? To what purpose is it if it is poisoned by a siege of suffering and of infirmity that cannot be eliminated, and that results in the dissolution of all that we cherish in life?

There are various ways of reacting to pain. One can suffer with rebellion. The man who does not believe and who does not pray suffers in this way even though he is silent. How many times, walking the corridors of hospitals, I have heard and even *seen* this terrifying silence! There are many people who shut up within themselves a sense of desperation, of rebellion, and of doubt without any sustaining comfort.

But there is another way of accepting suffering, the way of the man who believes in Christ and follows him. To suffer with love and for love! Not alone with patience, but with love . . . .

So long as the heart lives it is capable of this super-human act, which sums up our entire spirituality: to love. "O Lord, I cry, I suffer. I lie herein inert and unmoving; but I love You and I suffer for love of You."

DIALOGUES—POPE PAUL VI

WHAT THE CROSS SYMBOLIZES

Every time I look at the cross I am reminded of the greatness of God and the redemptive power of Jesus Christ. I am reminded of the beauty of sacrificial love and the majesty of unswerving devotion to truth. It causes me to say with John Bowring:

> In the cross of Christ I glory,
> Towering o'er the wrecks of time;
> All the light of sacred story
> Gathers round its head sublime.

It would be wonderful were I to look at the cross and sense only such a sublime reaction. But somehow I can never turn my eyes from that cross without also realizing that it symbolizes a strange mixture of greatness and smallness, of good and evil. As I behold that uplifted cross I am reminded not only of the unlimited power of God, but also of the sordid weakness of man. I think not only of the radiance of the divine, but also of the tang of the human. I am reminded not only of Christ at his best, but of man at his worst.

We must see the cross as the magnificent symbol of love conquering hate and of light overcoming darkness. But in the midst of this glowing affirmation, let us never forget that our Lord and Master was nailed to that cross because of human blindness. Those who crucified him knew not what they did.

MARTIN LUTHER KING, JR.

GOD ROAMS

A God as all-present and all-powerful and all-loving as the one proclaimed by the historic creeds is a God entitled to pick any lock and batter down any door. The fact that the creeds are true is no reason for assuming that God can and will work only through those who believe them to be true. God roams; He breaks; He enters; He is not above using an alias; He chooses and stations His witnesses where He will.

CHAD WALSH

THE TEMPTATIONS OF SAINT ANTHONY

Off in the wilderness bare and level
Anthony wrestled with the Devil.
Once he'd beaten the Devil down,
Anthony'd turn his eyes toward town
And leave his hermitage now and then
To come to grips with the souls of men.

Afterward, all the tales agree,
Wrestling the Devil seemed to be
Quite a relief to Anthony.

PHYLLIS MC GINLEY

33

A PRAYER FOR COURAGE

It takes *courage*
    to be crocus-minded.

Lord, I'd rather wait until June,
    like wise roses,
    when the hazards of winter are safely behind,
        and I'm expected,
        and everything's ready for roses.

But crocuses?
    Highly irregular.
    Knifing up through hard-frozen ground and snow,
        sticking their necks out,
    because they *believe* in spring
    and have something personal
        and emphatic to say about it.

Lord, I am by nature rose-minded.
    Even when I have studied the situation here
    and know there are wrongs that need righting,
    affirmations that need stating,
    and know also that my speaking out may offend —
        for it rocks the boat —
    well, I'd rather wait until June.
    Maybe later things will work themselves out,
    and we won't have to make an issue of it.

Lord, forgive.
   Wrongs don't work themselves out.
   Injustices and inequities and hurt don't
      just dissolve.

Somebody has to stick his neck out,
   somebody who cares enough
      to think through
      and work through hard ground,
   because he believes
   and has something personal
      and emphatic to say about it.

Me, Lord?
   Crocus-minded?
   Could it be that there are things that need
      to be said, and you want me to say them?
I pray for courage.
            Amen.

                        JO CARR AND IMOGENE SORLEY

HEROIC RELIGION

The church is like the Red Cross service in war time. It keeps life from degenerating into a consistent inhumanity, but it does not materially alter the fact of the struggle itself. The Red Cross neither wins the war nor abolishes it. Since the struggle between those who have and those who have not is a never-ending one, society will always be, in a sense, a battleground. It is therefore of some importance that human loveliness be preserved outside of the battle lines. But those who are engaged in this task ought to realize that the brutalities of the conflict may easily negate the most painstaking humanizing efforts behind the lines, and that these efforts may become a method for evading the dangers and risks of the battlefield.

If religion is to contribute anything to the solution of the industrial problem, a more heroic type of religion than flourishes in the average church must be set to the task. I don't believe that the men who are driven by that kind of religion need to dissociate themselves from the churches, but they must bind themselves together in more effective association than they now possess.

REINHOLD NIEBUHR

TREAT ME COOL, LORD

The "thous" and "didsts" of traditional prayers have little meaning today, especially for young people in trouble. To them, prayer in this kind of language has no relationship to the "gut issues" of life.

In order to help these disillusioned youngsters meet God on their own emotional turf, Chaplain Carl F. Burke of Buffalo's Erie County Jail has encouraged them to tell their real feelings to God. Some people may find the following prayers crude and even irreverent. But these words express the honest concerns of those who delivered them.

UNCERTAINTY

We wish we were sure
About you, God.
We want to believe —
But it's kinda hard.

Mostly hard to pray, Lord.
Kinda gives you the
Creeps to pray
And not be sure
Anyone's hearing.

LEARN ME HOW

Lord, I don't know all the big words the preacher sez.
I ain't much at talkin' to people and tell them what I'm
thinkin', but I'm in a mess now and need to know how
to talk to you. I hope you will learn me how.

SOME RICH, SOME POOR

Why did you make some rich people
And some poor people?
Why did I have to be a poor one?
If only we could have a couple of nice things.
And a few good days too!

HELP MOM

Mom is always sick
I wish you could help her
She is always bugged about something
And gets mad too quick
Maybe she drinks too much —
Can you help with that, God?

SOMETIMES

Sometimes, dear Jesus, we wish
Everything was cleaner
And not so dirty.

Sometimes we wish
We was real strong
When people bug us.

Sometimes we wish
We was true when we is
Scared of the big kids.

Sometimes we wish
We had
A bigger house.

Sometimes we wish
You were around here
More often, Jesus.

THE DIVINE DRAMA

Let us, in Heaven's name, drag out the Divine Drama from under the dreadful accumulation of slipshod thinking and trashy sentiment heaped upon it, and set it on an open stage to startle the world into some sort of vigorous reaction. If the pious are the first to be shocked, so much the worse for the pious — others will pass into the Kingdom of Heaven before them. If all men are offended because of Christ, let them be offended; but where is the sense of their being offended at something that is not Christ and is nothing like Him? We do Him singularly little honor by watering down His personality till it could not offend a fly. Surely it is not the business of the Church to adapt Christ to men, but to adapt men to Christ.

It is the dogma that is the drama — not beautiful phrases, nor comforting sentiments, nor vague aspirations to loving-kindness and uplift, nor the promise of something nice after death — but the terrifying assertion that the same God who made the world lived in the world and passed through the grave and gate of death. Show that to the heathen, and they may not believe it; but at least they may realize that here is something that a man might be glad to believe.

DOROTHY L. SAYERS

WHAT THE WORLD NEEDS NOW

There are certain things that our age needs, and certain things it should avoid. It needs compassion and a wish that mankind should be happy: it needs the desire for knowledge and the determination to eschew pleasant myths; it needs, above all, courageous hope and the impulse to creativeness. . . . The root of the matter is a very simple and old-fashioned thing, a thing so simple that I am almost ashamed to mention it for fear of the derisive smile with which wise cynics will greet my words. The thing I mean — please forgive me for mentioning it — is love, Christian love, or compassion. If you feel this, you have a motive for existence, a guide in action, a reason for courage, an imperative necessity for intellectual honesty.

BERTRAND RUSSELL

BOOM! *Sees Boom in Religion, too*

Atlantic City, June 23, 1957 (AP) — President Eisen-hower's pastor said tonight that Americans are living in a period of "unprecedented religious activity" caused partially by paid vacations, the eight-hour day, and modern conveniences.

"These fruits of material progress . . . have provided the leisure, the energy, and the means for a level of human and spiritual values never before reached."

Here at the Vespasian-Carlton, it's just one
religious activity after another; the sky
is constantly being crossed by cruciform
airplanes, in which nobody disbelieves
for a second, and the tide, the tide
of spiritual progress and prosperity
miraculously keeps rising, to a level
never before attained. The churches are full,
the beaches are full, and the filling-stations
are full, God's great ocean is full
of paid vacationers praying an eight-hour day
to the human and spiritual values, the fruits,
the leisure, the energy, and the means, Lord,
the means for the level, the unprecedented level,
and the modern conveniences, which also are full.
Never before, O Lord, have the prayers and praises
from belfry and phonebooth,
    from the ballpark and barbecue
the sacrifices, so endlessly ascended.

It was not thus when Job in Palestine
sat in the dust and cried, cried bitterly;
when Damien kissed the lepers on their wounds
it was not thus; it was not thus
when Francis worked a fourteen-hour day
strictly for the birds; when Dante took
a week's vacation without pay and it rained
part of the time, O Lord, it was not thus.

But now the gears mesh and the tires burn
and the ice chatters in the shaker and the priest
in the pulpit, and Thy Name, O Lord,
is kept before the public, while the fruits
ripen and religion booms and the level rises
and every modern convenience runneth over,
that it may never be with us as it hath been
with Athens and Karnak and Nagasaki,
nor Thy sun for one instant refrain from shining
on the rainbow Buick by the breezeway
or the Chris Craft with the uplift life raft;
that we may continue to be the just folks we are,
plain people with ordinary superliners and
disposable diaperliners, people of the stop'n'shop
'n'pray as you go, of hotel, motel, boatel,
the humble pilgrims of no deposit no return
and please adjust thy clothing, who will give to Thee,
if Thee will keep us going, our annual
Miss Universe, for Thy Name's Sake, Amen.

                              HOWARD NEMEROV

THE DANGER OF ABSOLUTE FAITH

There are similarities between absolute power and absolute faith: a demand for absolute obedience, a readiness to attempt the impossible, a bias for simple solutions — to cut the knot rather than unravel it, the viewing of compromise as surrender. Both absolute power and absolute faith are instruments of dehumanization. Hence, absolute faith corrupts as absolutely as absolute power.

ERIC HOFFER

RELIGION AND ETHICS

The belief in the Kingdom of God is the most difficult demand Christian faith makes of us. We are asked to believe in what seems impossible, namely in the victory of the spirit of God over the spirit of the world. Our trust and hope are invested in the miracle which the spirit can produce.

But the miracle must occur in us before it occurs in the world. We dare not hope that by our efforts we can create the conditions of the kingdom in the world. We must certainly work for it. But there can be no divine kingdom in the world, if there is not one first of all in our hearts. The beginning of the kingdom is to be found in our determination to bring our every thought and deed under the dominion of the kingdom. Nothing will come to pass without inwardness. The spirit of God will only contend against the spirit of the world when it has triumphed over the spirit in our hearts.

ALBERT SCHWEITZER

from RESISTANCE, REBELLION, AND DEATH

What I feel like telling you today is that the world needs real dialogue, that falsehood is just as much the opposite of dialogue as is silence, and that the only possible dialogue is the kind between people who remain what they are and speak their minds. This is tantamount to saying that the world of today needs Christians who remain Christians. . . . I shall not, as far as I am concerned, try to pass myself off as a Christian in your presence. I share with you the same revulsion from evil. But I do not share your hope, and I continue to struggle against this universe in which children struggle and die. . . . For a long time during those frightful [Nazi] years I waited for a great voice to speak up in Rome. I, an unbeliever? Precisely. For I knew that the spirit would be lost if it did not utter a cry of condemnation when faced with force. . . . What the world expects of Christians is that Christians should speak out, loud and clear, and that they should voice their condemnation in such a way that never a doubt, never the slightest doubt, could rise in the heart of the heart of the simplest man. That they should get away from

abstractions and confront the blood-stained face history has taken on today. The grouping we need is a grouping of men resolved to speak out clearly and to pay up personally. Possibly [Christianity] will insist on losing once and for all the virtue of revolt and indignation that belonged to it long ago. In that case Christians will live and Christianity will die.

ALBERT CAMUS

THE CHURCH AND CIVIL RIGHTS

I recall an ex-marine coming to the Youth Council. This young Black man had been three and one-half years in the marine corps, six months of which he spent fighting in Vietnam. When he came home, the young man and his wife sought a dwelling just two blocks beyond the ghetto area. The landlady, a gentle elderly woman, hesitated before telling them she had already rented the place. The young man's wife confronted the owner, asking, "It's because we're Negro that you won't rent to us, isn't it?" The landlady tried excusing herself in her reply. "Well, I can't rent to you. What would the people downstairs think? What will the neighbors say?"

This was during the Advent season. I could not help but think that this elderly woman had probably gone to church each Sunday of her life. And probably every Christmas, she had heard about Mary and Joseph and how there was no room for them in the inn. Perhaps she had even wept over their plight — snow falling, Mary pregnant, and no room in the inn. Yet religion had become so irrelevant to her that in the face of the young man at her own door she did not see the face of Joseph. In the face of his wife she could not see the face of Mary. It is in just such situations that Christianity is at its test. Either the Church becomes involved completely in the struggle for social justice, or the Church should close its doors because it has become like the Scribes and Pharisees whom Christ condemned, a whitened sepulchre.

JAMES E. GROPPI

TRAPS EVERYWHERE

In reading Chesterton, as in reading Macdonald, I did not know what I was letting myself in for. A young man who wishes to remain a sound Atheist cannot be too careful of his reading. There are traps everywhere — "Bibles laid open, millions of surprises," as Herbert says, "fine nets and stratagems." God is, if I may say it, very unscrupulous.

C. S. LEWIS

WHAT IS PRAYER?

There are regular word prayers.
We all know that kind.
   But there's more.
   A mother worrying about her son who isn't home
yet is praying.
   A man on his way to help out a kid in trouble
is praying.
   A man involved in his family, a real believer,
living and by this teaching his children
Your ways is praying.
   An airline hostess serving another is praying,
   and the man who reads the afternoon paper and
abhors the violence and feels compassion
for the suffering is praying.
   The kid who curses God,
   the beaten Negro who dares God,
   the priest or minister at his altar,
   the person where he is,
   the animal by his very being,
   all creation, life itself,
   all this is prayer and praying.
   Sometimes words are useless. But if we live
IN GOD, in You, Jesus, words are unnecessary
because then we are praying day and night,
in just being.
   It sounds deep, Jesus.
   But it is simple.
                                    CHRISTOPHER WILLIAM JONES

A TIME OF ECONOMIC DISTRESS

Eternal Spirit
Here in the quiet of thy sanctuary
We would not escape from life
Lo, how the silence of this place is populous with
    sound
The echoes of the footsteps of those
Who look for work and cannot find it
The cries of mothers
Anxious for their children's food
Disturb us; we beseech thee
By sounds of grief from the world outside
Let no one of us rest content
But make us penitent for our social evils
For our greed, selfish ambition, and carelessness
Of one another's good
O God, give us the grace
To open some channels
By which thy saving strength
Can come into the hearts of thy people
Grant us a new and holy indignation
Against social wrong
And above all, thy triple gift
Of faith and wisdom and courage.

HARRY EMERSON FOSDICK

53

JULY 19, 1961

Have mercy
Upon us.
Have mercy
Upon our efforts,
That we
Before Thee,
In love and in faith,
Righteousness and humility,
May follow Thee,
With self-denial, steadfastness, and courage,
And meet Thee
In the silence.

Give us
A pure heart
That we may see Thee,
A humble heart
That we may hear Thee,
A heart of love
That we may serve Thee,
A heart of faith
That we may love Thee,

Thou
Whom I do not know
But Whose I am.

Thou
Whom I do not comprehend
But Who hast dedicated me
To my fate.
Thou —

DAG HAMMARSKJÖLD

GOD IN THE WORLD

Christ is present in the world for both believer and nonbeliever. He is there whether we have faith in him or not, and before any religious words are spoken. He is Emmanuel, "God with us." He does not change the world into something it is not by his presence. It is still politics, still education, still business. He is there — in, with, and under the essential forms of the world. The manner of Christ's presence in worship thus opens our eyes to the way he is present in the world. He is there because he has chosen to be there, not because our piety or ceremonial bring him there. He was in the world before we were and will be there when we are gone. . . .

Thus God's presence in the human world does not cease because of a recession in the number or the piety of believers, or the passing of a style or religious language. God survives the post-Christian era because he does not need our theological formulations to conjure him into existence. The passing of the language of Zion merely means we must learn to speak to the world in its own terms. This means that we must listen, for God speaks to the church in the language of the world. Only when we have learned the world's language can we speak again of God. The world, its character, its hopes, its meaning, its destiny, becomes the *content* as well as the *context* of our speaking.

HARVEY COX

57

INDEX OF AUTHORS